Lead My

A Story of Pope John XXIII

by

BROTHER ROBERTO, C.S.C.

Illustrations by
Carolyn Lee Jagodits

DUJARIE PRESS

Notre Dame   Indiana

NIHIL OBSTAT

    C. F. Brooks, C.S.C.
      Censor Deputatus

CUM PERMISSU

    Brother Donatus Schmitz, C.S.C.
      Provincial

IMPRIMATUR

    ✠ Most Rev. Leo A. Pursley, D.D.
      Bishop of Fort Wayne

DEDICATION

to

Father Maurice Muller,
a young shepherd of souls

CHAPTER ONE

"I want you to take the sheep to the south pasture this afternoon, Angelo," Giovanni Roncalli told his oldest son. It was a warm day in the summer of 1890, and as he spoke, the man reached for his handkerchief, pulled it from the pocket of his patched trousers and mopped his brow.

"Yes, Papa," answered the boy, who would be nine years old on his next birthday, November 25.

"Take the dog with you," his father added. "Your mother is tired of having it under her feet all day and the animal will not learn to herd sheep any younger."

Angelo finished the last spoonful of vege-table soup, stuffed small pieces of sausage and bread inside his shirt for his afternoon lunch and rose from the table where he had eaten his midday meal. He said grace silently, blessed himself and hurried into the bright sunlight outside the wide door of the gray stone house.

"What did I do with my water jug?" he asked himself as he skipped happily across the sun-baked courtyard that hurt his bare feet. His dog came running up beside him as he hurried toward the well. He patted it briskly on the head, a sign of affection that caused the creature to wag its tail furiously and jump up on the youngster with wild delight.

"Oh, get down!" Angelo laughed. "I have to train you not to jump up and lick me like that."

After a quick search, Angelo found the

water jug and he was soon busy tugging at the bucket which had to be dropped deep into the well. He brought it up filled with bubbling, cold water, lifted it to his lips for a swallow and then poured until his jug gurgled to its full capacity.

"Come on," he called to his dog, lowering the bucket on its rope back into the well and moving in the direction of the sheepfold. He had little trouble letting the sheep out of their enclosure, but no sooner had he directed them on to the path that led to the lush south pasture than the dog, who knew little about the art of herding, ran to the front of the flock and began barking noisily at the leaders.

"Get away from them, you dumb animal!" Angelo yelled angrily. "Get away, or I'll take a stick to you! They're going in the right direction! What's the matter with you!"

Giovanni laughed as he watched his son's

activity with dog and flock. He stood in the shadowed doorway of his house for a few moments before returning to his work in the vineyards. "Our Angelo is having a little trouble training his sheep dog," he remarked over his shoulder to his wife.

Marianna came from the dark room and stood quietly beside her husband. "What did you expect?" she smiled as she watched. "That dog is one of the dumbest in all of northern Italy. Even our neighbors here at Sotto il Monte make funny remarks about its stupidity."

"Well, Angelo will train it in spite of its dullness," Giovanni said, "and I'll bet it will someday be a fine sheepherder."

"What is to become of Angelo in the fall?" Marianna asked suddenly. Her face was no longer smiling, and she looked sadly at the sturdy figure of the boy driving his flock across the broad plain before him. In the distance were blue and purple hills, foothills of the sky-piercing Alps. These were dotted with vine-yards and the quilt-patterns of wheat fields.

"He has finished his education here in the village school," Angelo's father mused. "Even his teacher and the parish priest admitted that he was a better-than-average student."

"But if he is to be a farmer like you, there is no need for him to continue his schooling."

"I don't want him to be a farmer. I want something better for our Angelo."

"He's our oldest son, Giovanni," his wife protested. "He is our future heir."

"What kind of heir?" her husband asked with a harsh laugh. "We are poor share-crop-pers! We have been share-croppers for genera-tions. The Roncallis will always be share-crop-pers. I want something better for Angelo. I want him to make a name for himself in this world."

Marianna was silent. For a moment she stood in the doorway and then turned back to her work in the kitchen in the midst of her daughters and younger children.

"Has it ever occurred to you that Angelo might be interested in studying for the priest-hood?" Giovanni called after her.

"He is a good boy. He prays much and has many virtues," Marianna said as she cleared the table. "But there are many farm boys like him in Italy and they do not go on to study for the priesthood. Where would we find the money to pay for his education if he wishes to become a priest?"

"We would have to work very hard, and we would have to pray even harder."

"Why don't you have a talk with the boy? Find out what he wants to be in life. Then, we can start making plans for his future."

Giovanni agreed. He pulled his cap down over his eyes to shade them from the sun and stepped out into the courtyard on his way back to the fields.

It was not long afterward on a cool, summer evening that father and son walked into the hills above the village of Sotto il Monte to discuss serious things. It did not come as a surprise to Giovanni that his gifted son wanted very much to continue his studies and eventually become a priest. "Instead of being a shepherd of sheep, I want to be a shepherd of souls," the boy said.

"You have a good mind, Angelo, and I know if your mother and I are able to finance your schooling in Celana, you will make the best use of your opportunities there."

"I already know a little Latin," Angelo admitted. "Father Nolis has taught me the grammar and we have read some of the Psalms in Latin."

"Then you have a good foundation for your classes in secondary school. You will have to walk back and forth to it every day, but that should not be too great a sacrifice if you are really interested in continuing your education."

"I will not mind walking," the boy said. "After all, you, yourself, once told me I came from very strong parents! Only a few hours after I was born, Mother was up and dressed and carrying me to church for baptism. And didn't you also tell me that I must have been sturdy to endure the four hours of waiting in the cold that day before the waters of the sacrament were splashed on my bald head?"

"That's right, Angelo," the man laughed as he walked along beside his son under the tall trees on the hillside. "You have a good memory. I shall do what I can to see that it is filled with the good things you still must learn."

And so it was decided that Angelo Roncalli

should continue his education—something which most of the other boys of his age and village were not able to do. In the fall, Angelo was enrolled in the school in Celana and the long two-hour journeys on foot began. Each morning he arose with the crowing of roosters and after a quick breakfast set off toward school. The road was poor and full of holes and stones and progress was slow. Tired from his journey, he had to sit for long hours at his desk listening to his teachers, taking notes on what he was told and reading from his books. Late afternoon found him trudging home where, after supper, he sat at the kitchen table in the light of a smoking candle to do his homework.

For a time all went well, but before many months had passed, the hard new life was beginning to have its effect on the sturdy youth. He grew pale and irritable and at last it was decided that his education must come to an end in

Celana.

"On your way to school today," his mother told him one morning, "I want you to take this letter to our parish priest."

"Should I wait for an answer?" the boy asked.

His mother shook her head and turned away from him in a way she had never done before. It was one of the few times in his life Angelo knew his mother was crying.

Upset and saddened, Angelo went off toward school carrying the letter in his hand. Anxious to know why it had caused his mother such sorrow, he decided to open and read it for himself before delivering it. He put his books down at the side of the road and carefully opened the letter.

"Reverend and dear Father," he read. "It is with deep sorrow that I must tell you that my husband and I think it best for our son, Angelo, to stop his schooling at Celana. The journey is so long and tiring for him that he can scarcely keep his eyes open in the evenings to do his homework. His health seems to be in danger also. Therefore, we think the time has come for him to give up plans for studying to be a priest and devote all of his time to farming."

"I am not giving up that easily!" Angelo told himself warmly, folding up the letter. His short, thick fingers grasped the white paper and before he had finished, he had torn the message into many small pieces. "I am going to continue my studies. I have been wasting my time and giving an impression I am not able to live this kind of life. It is time for me to show what I can do. I am going to become a priest and nothing is going to stop me!"

Angelo did not look back at the crumpled white flakes of paper lying at the side of the road. He did not bend to pick up stones as he walked toward Celana as was his custom. His lips moved in prayer and he hugged his books close to his ribs as he hurried along. He had made the first big decision of his life. It was to have amazing effects for him and for the world!

After finishing his classes in Celana, Angelo Roncalli sought for and obtained permission to enter the seminary in Bergamo, a city eight miles from his home. There in the fall of 1892 he became a seminarian. His rector told him to bring some money with him to pay for the day-to-day expenses there. Since there was little money at home, his mother went to members of her family to beg. She received very little and sadly returned home knowing that her son would have to work hard not only to master his new subjects, but also to pay the expenses he would incur at the seminary.

CHAPTER TWO

"I have been looking over your records from the secondary school in Celana," the Rector of the seminary in Bergamo told the new seminarian.

Angelo Roncalli shifted from one position to another on the uncomfortable chair in front of the priest's desk. The collar of his new cassock was too small for his husky neck and he pulled at it nervously as beads of perspiration began to form on his sun-tanned face. For a moment his brown eyes wore a worried look but then he saw the Rector smile, so he knew his record at the school must have been satisfactory.

"You did very well in languages, literature and history there," the priest went on. "I congratulate you. I hope you will be able to do as well here. You will have to continue your study of Latin and to that will be added Greek, philosophy, liturgy, Church law and Church history."

"I'll do my best," Angelo assured him.

"On free days you will be able to make short trips to places of pilgrimage. Your parents told me you liked to visit the shrines of Our Lady here in Bergamo and in the villages nearby. I think you should continue that custom."

"And during the summer vacations may I return to the farm to help my parents with the field work and the harvesting?"

"Of course," was the answer. "After long months over your books in these stuffy halls of learning, I think it would be the best thing in the world for you to get out into the hot sunshine for some exercise and hard work on the farm."

The young man knelt for the priest's blessing when the interview was over and then made his way back to his room to unpack his few belongings and prepare himself for the hard work of study that lay ahead.

Italy during the years that Angelo lived in the seminary was not a peaceful country. The government was anti-Catholic and did all in its power to hinder the bishops from carrying out their work of saving souls. Not a few prelates were arrested and kept in jail on the sole charge that they had obeyed orders from the pope! The seminarians during their walks and recreations talked about the unsettled condition of the times and Angelo spent considerable time on his knees in the chapel begging Our Lord in the Blessed Sacrament to help the Church in his land.

"We are fortunate to be living in Bergamo," Angelo told Giuseppe, one of his fellow seminarians, one day while they were walking briskly to the playground for recreation.

"What makes Bergamo so different from other cities of Italy?" his friend asked.

"Its bishop. Pope Leo XIII has written a wonderful letter called 'Rerum Novarum' which tells the bishops of the world about the true condition of the workingman. He doesn't just complain that the laboring classes are treated little better than slaves, but he has fine plans and advice for improving their condition."

"I've read the letter, but I don't see how Bishop Guindani has been able to do much to put its ideas into practice."

"Haven't you heard about the parish councils?" Angelo asked with a frown. "In a land where the Church is persecuted by the government, I think it is wonderful to have this means for sending information from bishop to people in the diocese without the government agents even knowing about it."

"But I thought all dioceses had systems like that," Giuseppe said with a shrug.

Angelo shook his head. "They don't, I'm sorry to say, and those few that do have copied the system from Bergamo. Also, the bishop has begun all kinds of societies to help the workers and farmers and poor. His advisors are intelligent lay people who know what the problems are and who are able to organize these societies and direct them so that the most good can be done for the greatest number of people."

"I can see you will certainly be a fighter for the rights of the poor and working classes after your ordination," his friend smiled as they reached the edge of the playing field.

"You bet I will!" Angelo smiled back. "But I'm not going to wait until then before starting to work. We can begin right now by praying for justice for them and for the success of the bishop's and pope's plans for them. Later we will be able to do more."

"Come on, Roncalli!" someone called from the ball field. "We want you on our side. We're losing the game and with those muscles of yours, we can even the score quickly."

Angelo waved to his friend and trotted off to join his team on the bright green field flooded with yellow sunshine.

For eight years Angelo Roncalli studied and prayed, worked and played in the seminary of Bergamo. The hot summers found him back on the farm at Sotto il Monte working with his brothers and sisters in the fields, but each fall he would return to Bergamo for further studies. He grew into a strong, handsome young man with tough muscles, a good mind and clear brown eyes that missed little and seemed always to be smiling.

One day in 1900 he was called to the office of the Rector. There he was told to sit down while the priest fumbled through a pile of papers on his desk.

"You have spent eight years with us here, Angelo," the rector began. "Are you still convinced that you wish to continue your studies for the priesthood?"

"Yes, Father. If I didn't have the conviction that God wants me to be a priest, I would have left here long ago to return to the farm."

"I am happy to hear that. Now I have a surprise for you. The professors here are quite pleased with your work. Oh, at the beginning, some of them were worried that you wouldn't make it because you had a rather poor background for classical studies and philosophy. But you have worked hard and your marks prove that. Your education here is finished now and we want you to take your four years of the study of theology in Rome."

"Rome?" the young man asked frowning. "I would not be able to scrape enough money together for the train ticket there much less the tuition at a seminary."

"Oh, don't worry about the money, Angelo," the priest laughed. "We are giving you a scholarship to study at the Roman Pontifical Seminary. Canon Cerasoli, who was once a canon in Rome and who was born and raised here in Bergamo, left money in his will for the purpose of having young, promising seminarians trained there at his expense. What do you think of the idea of traveling south for your theology?"

"I can't thank you enough, Father!" Angelo gasped. "I shall never be able to repay you!"

"That's what you think, young man! We

all look forward to great things from you, Roncalli. All of our administrators and bishops have been educated in Rome, so we think you may be on your way to higher things—maybe even the purple!"

"You flatter me. My ambition in life is to be a simple parish priest. If I ever succeed with the help of God's grace in becoming that, I shall be happy."

"I suggest you start packing at once," the priest told him as he rose from his chair and picked up an envelope from the top of his desk. "Here is your train ticket and a little money for incidental expenses on the way."

Overcome with joy, the young seminarian gratefully accepted the gift and then ran to tell his friends the good news.

In the Eternal City Angelo spent happy years sitting in the lecture halls of the seminary or poring over books in the different libraries or visiting different churches. In 1902 he spent a year in the army at Bergamo. On returning to Rome to complete his studies, he again found the narrow streets filled with noisy, playing children. People fascinated the young man and for hours he would visit with the children or the merchants in the public markets or the housewives standing in their narrow doorways. From each of these people he learned more about the conditions of the poor and the laborers, and to each he gave kind words, comfort or advice. Thus began a habit of meeting the people directly which he was to cultivate even until old age, and this trait was to make him one of the most beloved and easily approachable men in the world. No one was, is or will be afraid to approach Angelo Roncalli because his heart is big and warm and open to all who come to him.

On August 10, 1904, the young deacon was

ordained a priest by Bishop Ceppetelli in the church of Santa Maria in Monte Santo. The long years of preparation now seemed short to the young priest who had worked so hard and come so far in the pursuit of his vocation. His heart was full of joy when he gave his first blessing and received the congratulations of his fellow priests and friends.

"Where will you say your first Mass, Father Roncalli?" he was asked.

There was a twinkle in his dark eyes as he announced, "At the altar of the Confession in St. Peter's—right above the tomb of the first Pope."

"How did you ever manage to receive such a privilege?"

The priest smiled and shook his head. "It is a secret, but I can tell you this. The first pope was a humble fisherman and I am sure he would have no objection to a young priest who comes from the farm saying his first Mass over his grave. We have a humble origin in common."

Father Roncalli lost no time in leaving Rome to return to his home in northern Italy. Too poor to travel to Rome for his ordination and first Mass, his parents and many relatives and friends were eagerly awaiting his return. They were all at the station to meet him and typical of warm Italian welcomes, they showered his newly consecrated hands with kisses.

His second Mass was said not in his parish church of St. John the Baptist which was then being repaired, but in another church not far from the village. After the Mass, as the priest was leaving the church in the midst of his family, he caught sight of his old friend, the doctor.

The two men shook hands and then the doctor smiled and said, "So you are a priest at last, Angelo! Congratulations! It would not surprise me at all if the cardinals someday elect you pope in Rome!"

The young priest laughed, thinking it was a good joke and never dreaming that he would oneday sit on the throne of St. Peter to rule the entire Catholic world. "I shall be quite happy as a parish priest in some little hamlet of this diocese," he chuckled.

"Do you know what your first assignment will be?" the doctor asked.

Angelo shook his head. "I have a short vacation here at home and then I must return to Rome."

"Good luck to you, Father," the doctor said.

"Thank you. Aren't you coming over to the Roncalli farm for the reception?" he asked.

"Perhaps later," was the reply. "One of the ladies in the neighborhood is expecting a baby and I must visit her now."

"Well, come when you can," said the priest.

"The door is always open."

The Roncallis went off glowing with pride and joy in their son who had at last reached the highest dignity that can be granted a human being—the power to consecrate bread and wine into the Body and Blood of the God-man, to administer the Sacraments and to preach the Gospel.

It was not long after the vacation of Father Roncalli and his return to Rome that the old bishop of Bergamo died. Pope St. Pius X consecrated with his own hands one of the most famous priests in all of Italy as the new bishop of Bergamo. He was Bishop Radini-Tedeschi and this remarkable man was to play a most important role in the future life of the young zealous priest.

The new bishop had worked for years to help the Church in Italy against the hostile government. "I am sending you to Bergamo," the saintly pope told him after his consecration, "because it is the most important diocese in Italy and much has been done there for Catholic Action and for the laboring people."

"I shall need a secretary to help me with my work there."

"Surely there is some young priest from Bergamo who can serve you in this position. I thought those two young priests who served at the altar during your consecration were from Bergamo," the pope said.

The bishop soon discovered that one of the priests to whom the pope had referred was Father Roncalli. The bishop interviewed the twenty-two-year-old cleric, offered him the post of secretary and joyfully received his acceptance.

"I shall be happy to help you," Father Roncalli told him, and thus began his first assignment.

CHAPTER THREE

"My life here in Bergamo will not always be peaceful and quiet, Father Roncalli," Bishop Radini-Tedeschi told his secretary soon after they had arrived in the bishop's palace and begun their work together. "For twenty years I have been active in Catholic movements all over Italy and although I lived in the Vatican, I traveled everywhere in order to attend meetings, organize societies and meet the leaders of the different conferences who were busy winning back from the state what the Church had lost to it."

"I have often heard you were a good fighter,

Your Excellency," Father Roncalli smiled, "and I, myself, like a good fight when it is for the right cause. Knowing how the Church has been persecuted in this country and how its rights and privileges have been disregarded, I shall be more than happy to help you in any way I can in carrying on the work of Catholic Action."

"I hope you enjoy traveling, Father," the bishop remarked, "because we will probably go to many different places. My enemies consider me one of the biggest windbags of this age, and in a way I suppose they are right. Over a period of twenty years, I have given more than twelve hundred major speeches! I am not one to keep my mouth shut when the truth must be spoken loudly and clearly. So, have your suitcase handy at all times. You will never know when you must come with me on the spur of the moment for a trip or a lecture tour."

"I shall be ready," Father Roncalli said remembering that his bishop had on several occasions been chosen by Pope Leo XIII to go to capitals of Europe as his delegate in handling delicate diplomatic affairs.

It was from his learned and remarkable bishop that Father Roncalli learned the fine art of diplomacy and how to deal with every type of person from the lowliest to the highest. From him also he learned the value of constant study and research, and later the priest made use of this in writing various books.

When the bishop actively joined workers who went on strike in Ranica and learned that some of them were unable to support their families because their means of income had been cut off, he sent them money and aid so that they could continue the strike in order to win the right to organize into unions.

"Didn't Pope Leo tell the world that workers have the right to organize in his letter twenty years ago?" the bishop asked one evening after a hectic day.

Father Roncalli nodded his agreement.

"Then why does it take so long to put his words into effect? The capitalists do not want the workers to organize and defend their rights in Ranica. Since there is no other way to win this right, the workers must continue the strike until their wishes are granted. A principle is at stake here, and we must be willing to shed our blood for a principle if such drastic action is necessary."

For seven weeks the strike dragged on before the workers won their right to organize unions. "I am glad it is over," the bishop said wearily when he heard the news. "I suppose you know that several people complained to the pope about my taking sides with the workers."

"Why did they do that?" the secretary

asked.

"They didn't understand what was at stake, I suppose."

"Are you going to tell the pope why you helped the workers?"

"There is no need to do so," he replied. "I already have a letter from him. He told me he did not disapprove of what I did. He knew that I was close to the situation and knew it in all its aspects. So the matter is closed."

"You once told me that we would have fights here," the priest said with a sigh of relief.

"There will be more, but now that you have had your baptism of fire, you will not find the others so trying. I am used to them after all these years."

Because of his many activities, Bishop Radini-Tedeschi had to budget his time carefully, and early in their work together, he suggested that his young secretary do the same thing. "I think you should do some teaching at the seminary, too, Father," the bishop suggested one day shortly before the fall term began. "They tell me you were quite a scholar in Rome. It would be a shame to have all that learning go to waste here in Bergamo when it could be used in teaching future priests."

"I think I would enjoy teaching," Father Roncalli told him, "but on what subjects would I have to lecture?"

"Church history and apologetics."

"I have always enjoyed the study of history. By having to teach it to the seminarians, I could continue my study of it."

"Then, you will accept the position?"

"I shall find a place for it on my schedule," the secretary replied. "I have drawn up a plan for the careful use of my time as you suggested. Using the plan, I find I have much more time than I thought for the things I wish to do."

Father Roncalli found great joy in teaching the young seminarians. He unpacked his many notebooks which he had brought from Rome and began to reread them. The works he had studied in Church history by Cardinal Baronius he read again, and the notes he had taken on the life of the famous scholar now turned up among his papers.

After much thought about the matter over a long period of time, he went to see the bishop.

"You look tense tonight, Angelo," the prelate greeted him. "What's on your mind?"

"Would you think I was crazy if I told you I want to write a book?"

"Of course not! What do you want to write about?"

"I have a lot of notes on Cardinal Baronius, the historian. I have been interested in his life and work for a long time, and now I would like to write a book about him so that more people may come to know and love him."

"Didn't he follow St. Philip Neri as head of the Oratorians?" the bishop asked.

Father Roncalli nodded, "And he was quite a saintly man himself."

"Go ahead and start working on your book," the bishop urged. "I'll do all I can to help you publish it."

The bishop's secretary felt that a great load had been removed from his shoulders and he hurried back to his room to begin the hard work of writing. He soon discovered that writing is a very time-consuming job, and since he had to travel much with the bishop, take care of his letters and files as well as lecture in the seminary, there were times when he wondered if he would ever finish the biography.

By devoting every spare moment to his manuscript, the priest was finally able to finish his book, and aided by the bishop, he had the joy of seeing it published in 1908. That the life and thoughts of Cardinal Baronius had a profound influence on the young priest is evident from the fact that he chose as his motto as pope, the Cardinal's motto: Obedience and Peace.

Not long after finishing his first book, Father Roncalli was called to the bishop's office and told to prepare for a journey to Milan. "We must meet Cardinal Ferrari there to make plans for a council of Church leaders that will soon be held. Oh, and take plenty of notebooks along with you. I intend to introduce you to the head librarian of the Ambrosian Library there. I think you will find Father Ratti a very interesting person. He will show you many books that will be valuable in your lectures on Church history."

Between meetings with the cardinal and bishops in Milan, Father Roncalli was able to spend much time in the Ambrosian Library. His first meeting with Father Ratti, who was one day to rule the Church as Pope Pius XI, was memorable.

"While brousing through the archives," the secretary told the librarian, "I found thirty-nine volumes which greatly interested me."

Father Ratti raised his eyebrows and asked, "What were they?"

"The Spiritual Archives of Bergamo," was the answer. "In glancing through them, I found a detailed history of my diocese and also papers from the visit and inspection that was made there in 1575 by St. Charles Borromeo. I would like to study those volumes carefully and then write a book about my findings. I'm sure the testimony and history of the period would be interesting. There are accounts of trials and reports of spies in the midst of all that material."

"It would be a fine study to make—especially for a man who is young. Those thirty-nine volumes weigh hundreds of pounds and just imagine how long it would take to read them, take notes, and then bring the findings together into a readable book!"

"It would probably take many years to finish the work, but do you think I should consider it?"

"Yes, I do," Father Ratti told him, "and I will help you by having all the correspondence photographed for you, since documents of that kind cannot be removed from the archives."

By the time bishop and secretary were ready to return to Bergamo, Father Ratti had prepared all the material the young priest would need for his research.

"Are you moving the entire Ambrosian Library back to Bergamo?" Bishop Radini-Tedeschi teased when he saw the boxes to be shipped.

"Only a large part of it," Father Roncalli teased. "Father Ratti insisted that I take all this material."

"I'll have to appoint a commission of people to help you with this work. You won't be able to finish it by yourself in a hundred years—and I doubt that you will live that long!"

True to his word, the bishop appointed professors from the seminary to help his secretary in his research, but before long, Father Roncalli found that he was doing the work alone. After long years and hard work, he succeeded in finishing his monumental study of the visitation of St. Charles Borromeo to Bergamo and in 1936, when the first of its five volumes was published, he sent an autographed copy to Pope Pius XI who had helped him so much. Not until 1959 was the fifth volume published thus bringing to an end the work that had begun fifty years before.

CHAPTER FOUR

For ten years, Father Roncalli acted as
Bishop Radini-Tadeschi's secretary. His life
was a busy and prayerful one lived in imitation
of the holy bishop he served. "He was my great
spiritual father," he later admitted. "In him
I found a star that could guide me in all my
actions. He was a saintly man who fought
bravely for what he knew to be right."

On August 22, 1914, Father Roncalli found
himself kneeling by the bedside of the dying
bishop. The prelate had been anointed and as
his end drew near, he found it hard to breathe.

"I never told you this, Angelo," he whis-

pered to the priest at his side, "but Pope Pius X, who died two days ago, told me after he consecrated me bishop that he would come for me soon after his death to take me to heaven so that we could be together there forever."

"Do you think he is coming so soon?"

"Yes," came the tired whisper. "He is keeping his promise."

Suddenly the bishop could not catch his breath, and the priest lifted him up from the pillows and held him somewhat erect. There was a deep sigh and then the holy prelate breathed out his soul to God. Gently the strong arms of Father Roncalli settled the exhausted body back on the pillows. The dark head of the young priest fell and for a long time he wept there alone.

After the funeral of his dear friend, Father Roncalli was numb with loneliness and undecided about his future. "All my friends are going to war," he complained one day to one of his fellow teachers at the seminary.

"I know, Father. It is a pity. Even the seminarians and priests are being drafted."

"Then, I suppose it is only a matter of time until we are summoned to the ranks. I served as a soldier in 1902 during my seminary studies, and since I worked up to the rank of a sergeant, no doubt I too will be called into the medical corps with the rest."

"That is where most of the priests serve, and it is a good place for them. They are at the side of the doctors during and after the battles. They can administer the last Sacraments to the soldiers whom the doctors cannot help."

By Pentecost of 1915, Father Roncalli had received his notice to report to the hospital of St. Ambrose in Milan for further instructions. He was given his old rank of sergeant, a drab uniform and a heavy military cape.

"Sergeant Roncalli!" the officer in charge of the hospital announced when he reported for duty. "You are to return to Bergamo. There is a military hospital there which is in need of a chaplain. You will be able to care for the spiritual needs of the wounded and dying."

Sergeant Roncalli returned the crisp salute of the officer and turned sharply to leave. He must have smiled as he left the room, for he had come from Bergamo only to be told to return to it at once. It would have saved him time and money if the army had sent the order by letter to stay where he was. But the Italian army did not act so efficiently and before long the sergeant was to learn it did not act very efficiently on the battle field either.

Day by day the priest remained in the military hospital. Early each morning he said Mass in the chapel and then carried the Blessed Sacrament to the men who wished to receive

Holy Communion. The rest of the day was spent in visiting the different wards. It caused him great pain to see young men brought in from the battle fields bleeding and broken, mumbling fragments of sentences that meant nothing.

For each of those in agony, he had a smile and a word of comfort, and when the doctor's nod told him there was little hope of saving the young man's life, Father Roncalli would give a last absolution and prepare to administer Extreme Unction.

After long months on duty in the hospital, Father Roncalli was allowed to return home for a brief furlough.

"What have you done to yourself?" his sister, Assunta, asked in horror when she caught sight of him.

"Don't you like my regulation uniform?"

"It's not the uniform, Angelo," she said

breaking out laughing, "it's . . . it's that . . . ridiculous mustache!"

"What's wrong with my mustache?" he asked pretending to be insulted by her laughter. "I think it makes me look very distinguished."

"Oh, for heaven's sake!" giggled his sister, "you look just terrible! Come on in here," she said motioning him into the house for other members of the family to see the monstrosity. "They will die laughing at you!"

Good-natured Angelo laughed with them and then admitted that he grew the gay, dark mustache in a moment of weakness. "I'll shave it off now," he said, "because I have just been made a lieutenant in the army and official chaplain at the military hospital in Bergamo."

During his four years of military service, Father Roncalli used every spare moment to further his writing of the life of St. Charles Borromeo. Sometimes until late at night, he pored over his books written in old Latin and in the ancient Italian dialect of the district. The scholar in him could not be killed even by a war with its heart-breaking period of helping dying soldiers. When the five volumes were finally finished, he began to collect notes on the life of his friend, Bishop Radini-Tadeschi, and before long he was hard at work on a life of the man who had done more than any other to make him a good priest and an excellent scholar.

"Will you please come back to the seminary for a series of lectures on apologetics?" the Rector begged him one day.

"It would be very difficult for me to do that, Father," he told him. "Look at all these bedridden soldiers," and as he spoke, he motioned up and down the long aisles of the hospital ward. "I am free only in the late afternoons and evenings."

"Come then, please. The seminarians have been asking to hear you again."

"That is very kind of them," the priest said, deeply touched by their devotion to their old teacher. "I shall look forward to seeing them again. I will have to dig up my notes, but I will come as soon as I can."

The priest kept his promise and the lectures began. They had not gone on long, however, before the teacher noticed that the class was becoming smaller and smalled. "Where are all the boys who began with us?" he asked one night.

"They have been drafted," was the reply.

"I am sorry to hear that," the priest said, "but we shall go on until there is no one left for the lectures." When that time came, the teacher opened his portfolio and handed out his much-thumbed notes to the last few young men taking the course. "Read these notes at your leisure, dear friends," he said sadly. "Perhaps when the was is over, we shall meet here again."

The war finally came to an end and slowly the seminarians drifted back from the army to take up their studies for the priesthood once more. Many did not return. They had given their lives on the battle field together with some of the priests whom Father Roncalli had known. The war had taken its bitter and heavy toll, and those who survived had to work all the harder to repair the evils it had caused.

"I have much work for you to do," Bishop Marelli told the priest after summoning him for an interview. "You used to teach Church history and apologetics at the seminary here in Bergamo did you not?"

"Yes, Your Excellency, when I was the bishop's secretary."

"From now on, I want you to devote all your time to giving spiritual direction to the theology students. That is far more important work than teaching since it involves the forming of priest's souls."

"I know," the priest admitted, "and I feel very unworthy to do such work."

"Nonsense!" the bishop snorted. "You are well qualified for it. If I didn't think so, I would not allow you to do it."

"May I ask your permission for a project I have long wished to put into effect?"

"What is that?"

"I would like to open a student center here for the poorer boys who are studying in the state schools in the city. They need protection and advice and a place to live."

"Where would you open such a center?"

"In the old Marenzi Palace. The building can be rented cheaply and it is big enough for the work I would like to do for the young."

"Go ahead with the project," the bishop

said enthusiastically. "You have my blessing. If I can ever be of assistance, simply call on me."

The priest knelt for the prelate's blessing and then hurried away. He had much work to do. Both his work as spiritual director and founder of the student center were highly successful. This was due to the fact that he prayed much and depended on God for help after doing all in his power to carry on the work.

Father Roncalli was a man who paid close attention to everything—even the smallest details. When the students saw a large mirror hanging on the landing of the stairs they used to reach their rooms, they laughed and pointed to the inscription below it.

"What does it say?" someone called from the top of the stairs soon after the mirror had been hung there.

"It says, 'Know yourself!' and guess who put it up for us?"

"Father Roncalli, of course."

"I don't blame him. It is his nice way of saying that we have been leaving the house to go to class or parties looking very unkempt. From now on we can see how we look by glancing in the mirror."

"At least our hair can be combed and our clothes brushed," one of the students admitted.

Thus quietly and effectively, the gentle priest made his point, and after that the students he cared for were always seen leaving the house neat and clean.

Remembering the good work of Bishop Radini-Tedeschi in the field of Catholic Action, Father Roncalli continued to devote much of his time to different Catholic societies in Bergamo. He became a leader in the field because he had long studied its history and taken great interest in it since his days in the seminary.

His hard work was to bear rich fruit and its

effects were called to the attention of Pope Benedict XV in Rome. In December of 1920, the Pope sent a special message to Father Roncalli inviting him to come to Rome and asking him to devote his talent to the study of the Catholic missions. The Society for the Propagation of the Faith was in need of reorganization. The pope hoped that the zealous priest from Bergamo would carry out this task for him.

"I have come to say good-bye," Father Roncalli told his bishop during their last interview.

"So you are being called to the Vatican!" the prelate smiled. "Well, if you do half as good a job there as you have done here, you will have the Church's missions well-cared for in very short time."

"I'm afraid the work won't be that easy," the priest smiled. "There will always be need for more missionaries and more money for their projects in different parts of the world."

"I suppose. We shall miss you very much, but we are sure to hear great things from you in Rome."

The bishop was right. Almost as soon as he arrived in the Eternal City, Father Roncalli was sent on important missions throughout Europe. His reputation as an organizer and diplomat was becoming well known in important circles in the Vatican, but no one could guess what plans God had for this happy, hard-working little man.

Happy to be back in Rome after long years in northern Italy, Father Roncalli was soon sent off on tours of inspection to Holland, Belgium, France and Germany. Everywhere he saw the ruins caused by the war and everywhere he learned how much the Church needed priests and zealous lay people to rebuild the broken countries of Europe.

Returning to Rome with much information

which his sharp eyes and ears had gathered for the Vatican, he was made president of Italy's section of the Society for the Propagation of the Faith. In May, 1921, he was handed a letter. He opened it and read it at once.

It told him that the Pope was pleased with his work for the Society. He was named a Monsignor and thus became a Domestic Prelate of the papal court. The humble priest shook his head and frowned. He could not understand why this honor had been conferred upon him.

The words of Bishop Marelli were indeed coming true. Great things were expected of Angelo Roncalli and great things were happening to him.

CHAPTER FIVE

After the death of Pope Benedict XV in 1922, Cardinal Ratti came to the throne of St. Peter and chose the name, Pope Pius XI. The former librarian at the Ambrosian Library in Milan did not forget his old friend, Monsignor Roncalli. He made him a member of the Pontifical Society for the Propagation of the Faith whose task it was to reorganize and modernize the whole Society for the welfare of the Church throughout the world. He was also given a special assignment: to prepare a Missionary Exhibition for the Holy Year of 1925. As if such duties were not enough for him, he

was also named Professor at the Roman Seminary and had to devote much time to the preparation and presentation of lectures on the lives and works of the early Fathers of the Church.

The Missionary Exhibition prepared by Monsignor Roncalli required much planning and work and when it was finally displayed early in 1925, everyone in Rome who visited it was pleased. Pope Pius XI had taken much interest in the project and now praised the man who had made it possible. On March 3, he surprised him by appointing him Archbishop of Areopolis and Apostolic Visitor to the country of Bulgaria.

On the feast of St. Joseph, Angelo Roncalli was consecrated Archbishop in the church of San Carlo and went to say his first Mass as prelate at the altar of the Confession in St. Peter's basilica where he had once said his first Mass as a priest.

"I am sending you to Bulgaria," the Pope told the new Archbishop, "because I want you to do much work there for me. Judging from the fine work you have done here in Rome, I believe you are the best man for this assignment. I want you to investigate the conditions of Catholics in all parts of Bulgaria. This will not be an easy task because the country is now in a state of unrest. Local revolutions are common and the communists are said to be sending in many secret agents to stir up more disorder. There may be many groups of Catholics who are without priests or bishops. If this is so, you must tell me in your reports and make suggestions as to who would be the best priests to be elevated to bishoprics in the different regions."

"I shall do my best for you, Your Holiness," the archbishop said, and when the interview was at an end, he knelt to receive the papal blessing. He was escorted from the pope's presence and before long was on his way to his first important diplomatic mission for the Vatican. Thus began a period of twenty-seven years of travel and work which was to take him to many places to help many people. He smilingly called himself, "God's traveler" and had to be ready at a moment's notice to leave an old post for a new one and a more important one.

It did not take Archbishop Roncalli long to discover what the conditions of Catholics in Bulgaria were. He knew in a short time that what was needed most by these people was an able administrator. After a long period of prayer and thought, he sent to Pope Pius XI the name of a young priest, Father Kurteff, to be named to this important post. For years this remarkable man was to work as Exarch in Bulgaria and only after long years at his task of ministering to souls was he to be imprisoned by the communists together with other bishops whom Roncalli had proposed for various dioceses.

Before a year had passed, the papal visitor had determined how many Catholics lived in the country and what their most pressing needs were. He proposed the much-needed reorganization that was necessary and was delighted to learn that the pope agreed wholeheartedly with him and quickly set up new dioceses for the people without leaders.

To train future priests, a seminary was founded, and the archbishop brought Jesuit priests to staff it. Seeing that education was at a low ebb among the people, he established a series of Catholic schools and also began Catholic Action groups in various cities.

The visitor worked hard and prayed much in order to bring order out of chaos in the country of Bulgaria. Pope Pius XI was delighted with the results of his visit and decided to make him Apostolic Delegate to that country. "Your former position was only a temporary one," the pope told him, "but since you have done such good work, I want you to remain there permanently to bring to its full flower the important work for the Church which you have begun."

When King Boris III of Bulgaria invited Archbishop Roncalli to his palace, the prelate went at once to visit him.

"As you know," the King told him, "I am a member of the Orthodox Church and I am engaged to Princess Giovanna of Savoy who is a Roman Catholic."

"I know, Your Majesty," the archbishop nodded. "I have read the newspaper reports of your forthcoming marriage."

"I wish to know the conditions to which I must agree before the marriage can take place."

"Since this will be a mixed marriage, you will have to promise in writing that only the

Roman Catholic wedding ceremony will take place. There can be no ceremony here in Sofia in the Orthodox cathedral."

"I understand."

"Then, also, you must promise that any children who may be born to you and the princess will be baptized and raised as Roman Catholics."

"I shall be glad to make those promises," the king said. "Will you prepare the necessary documents and bring them to me as soon as possible?"

"I shall be happy to do that for you," the archbishop agreed good-naturedly.

After the documents had been signed and the wedding of the king and princess had taken place in Assisi, trouble began. Soon after his return to Sofia, the king made it clear that his promises meant nothing. He ordered a second wedding ceremony to take place in the Orthodox cathedral. Archbishop Roncalli protested this action warmly and recalled to the king his written promise. Later when children were born to the royal couple, they were taken for baptism to the Orthodox cathedral.

Taking matters into his own hands, Archbishop Roncalli went directly to the queen and learned from her that she was powerless to oppose her husband. After discovering that the king, alone, was responsible for the broken pledges, the archbishop sent his report to Rome where the pope firmly condemned the king's actions before a meeting of cardinals. He sent a message of sympathy to the queen who had nothing to do with the incidents and marveled at the ability of Archbishop Roncalli who carried out his work in this difficult problem and at the same time remained on friendly terms with the king whom he had to scold for his broken promises.

Pleased with his long years of service in Bulgaria, Pope Pius decided to send his diplomat as Apostolic Delegate to Turkey and Greece. In January of 1935, the Archbishop arrived in Istanbul to take up his new tasks.

One day shortly after he came to Istanbul, Archbishop Roncalli went shopping. After long hours in bookshops and market places of the city, he returned with several bundles. He unwrapped each of his treasures while his secretary looked on in admiration.

"What are all those books?" the young priest asked him.

"I learned to speak Bulgarian in Bulgaria," the prelate smiled, "and now I have bought some Turkish, Greek and Russian grammars so that I can learn these languages. I also found some excellent books on Orthodox beliefs which I wish to study. We must do all in our power to unify the Church. Someday, by the grace of God, I hope that all Christians will return to the Roman Catholic Church. In the meantime, I am going to learn all I can about the beliefs of the people here in the Near East."

With his usual zeal and hard work, the Archbishop acquired much knowledge about the Orthodox Church. The day was to come when he would be able to use that vast fund of information in his efforts to bring about unity of Christians. As pope, he would oneday call a great Council of the Church in an attempt to unify the Christian sects of the entire world.

While visiting Athens, Archbishop Roncalli went in person to visit different Catholic communities. He was kind to members of Orthodox churches and encouraged them in their cultural and charitable works. Alarmed at the growing influence of communism in the Middle East, the prelate watched in horror as one country after another fell prey to this new, godless way of life.

When the Nazis swept over Greece during World War II, the Apostolic Delegate did much to help the conquered people. When asked for aid by members of the government, the archbishop hurried to Rome for an audience with Pope Pius XII. With the help of the pope, he was able to have supplies shipped to the starving Greeks. The allies agreed to open their blockade for this purpose and before long ships carrying food, clothing and medicine were steaming into Greek harbors.

When he learned that thousands of Jews were being deported from Greece by the Nazis, he protested loudly against such brutal tactics. He was powerless to help them because his protests were ignored. The Jews, however, were never to forget his efforts on behalf of their welfare.

CHAPTER SIX

One December evening in 1944 shortly before the end of the war, Archbishop Roncalli was handed a telegram from the Vatican. Because his secretary was out, he decided to decode the message himself. He did so several times before he was sure he had made no mistake. He was ordered to return to Rome at once. He was to be transferred to Paris as Papal Nuncio.

In Rome when he protested that he was not capable of doing the work in France, he was told that the pope had made the decision and he had full confidence in the new Nuncio.

On January 1, 1945, Archbishop Roncalli stood at the head of the diplomatic corps to address Charles de Gaulle, head of the government. Had he not arrived in time, an address would have been given by the Russian ambassador, whose speech had been prepared for him in Moscow.

For eight years the Nuncio was to remain in Paris doing his difficult work quietly and well. During this time he was to become one of the best-loved men in that country. When the government demanded that thirty-three bishops be removed from their dioceses because they had worked with the Vichy government which had cooperated with the Nazis during the war, the Nuncio demanded a full investigation and succeeded in having charges dropped against thirty of them.

As each new problem arose, the archbishop tried to find a solution for it. He continued his long walks in Paris as he had done in the other cities to which he had been sent. He liked to travel and enjoyed visits with every class of people. He learned to speak fluent French.

Four years after the war when German prisoners of war were still being held in French camps, Archbishop Roncalli did much to obtain their release and their return home. He always pointed out the difference between the German people, themselves, and their Nazi government. He helped Catholic schools throughout the country and served for a time as the pope's observer of UNESCO.

On January 12, 1953, Pope Pius XII made Archbishop Roncalli a cardinal and following an old tradition, the Nuncio to Paris received his red biretta from the hands of President Auriol of the French Republic. Auriol was a Socialist and an unbeliever, but he was a close friend of the new cardinal and at his suggestion had invited the mayor of Sotto il Monte and several peasants from Cardinal Roncalli's native village to the palace for the ceremony. Even when raised to the status of a prince of the Church, the humble cardinal did not forget his old friends in northern Italy.

Only three days after he received the red hat, Cardinal Roncalli was appointed Patriarch of Venice, a position once held by Pope St. Pius X before his election to the papacy.

"You will not find that I am a diplomat or an important person," he told his people after he arrived by gondola in the square before the gorgeous cathedral of St. Mark. "But in me you will find a simple parish priest. Come to me at any time. I am here to help you."

The delighted Venetians took him at his word and it was not long before they were crowding to his palace to see him. When his secretaries objected that these people were taking up too much of his time, he merely smiled and said, "Some of these people may wish to go to confession. I must always be available to them for that reason."

While strolling through a hotel lobby one day on one of his many walks, the cardinal spotted President Auriol, his old friend from Paris. He greeted him warmly and insisted on taking him to his palace for a tour and visit. He took pride in pointing out the room once used by Pope St. Pius X while he was patriarch. It was very simply furnished and the president remarked about it.

"He came from a poor family, as I did," the cardinal said, "and people like that do not need many things for their rooms."

Many important visitors came to Venice while Cardinal Roncalli headed the diocese and on one occasion, he enjoyed taking Cardinal Wyszynski of Poland for a tour of the city in a gondola. When Cardinal Feltin came from Paris to visit, the patriarch took him through the cathedral of St. Mark and together they attended Vespers. As they were leaving the cathedral, they heard a band playing in the square.

"Come on," the cardinal smiled, leading his guest across to the band stand. He applauded the musicians warmly when they had finished their selection and then whispered something into the director's ear. The man smiled, nodded and ordered his musicians to change the order of their music. Before long the strains of the French national anthem were filling the air and Cardinal Roncalli smiled and stood at attention beside his friend from Paris.

He did much to encourage the composition of fine modern music by allowing the cathedral of St. Mark to be used for the performance of music by Igor Stravinsky during the International Music Festival. In 1956, he again brought Stravinsky to Venice for the performance of his beautiful "Sacred Canticle to Honor the Name of St. Mark." Each year he went to visit the art exhibits in the local galleries and to the surprise of many, he stoutly announced that he liked some of the modern paintings he saw there.

He continued to travel widely and in 1958 flew in a jet plane to Lourdes as the pope's personal representative to dedicate the basilica over the famous grotto.

When Pope Pius XII died on October 9, 1958, Cardinal Roncalli was summoned to Rome for the Pontiff's funeral and the selection of a new pope. Standing on the platform in Venice before boarding the train, the cardinal told his people that he hoped to return to them after two weeks.

His wish was not to be granted. On October

28, after the twelfth ballot, Cardinal Roncalli was elected pope. White smoke went up as the ballots were burned and radios carried the news all over the world: "We have a Pope: Angelo Joseph Roncalli!" The name chosen by the new pontiff was Pope John XXIII, and he later explained that he chose it because it was his father's name, his parish church in Sotto il Monte had been named after St. John the Baptist, and his cathedral of St. John Lateran bore that name.

Sitting at their radios in northern Italy to hear the wonderful news were the new pope's brothers and sister, Alfredo, Giuseppe, Saverio and Assunta. Weeping for joy, they received the congratulations of their neighbors and then began to make preparations for the long journey to Rome to witness their brother's coronation.

CHAPTER SEVEN

In his first message to the world, Pope John XXIII greeted all of the sheep of his huge flock throughout the world from cardinals to the poor and persecuted. He prayed for those who are enslaved, for the Eastern Church and for all who are separated from the Catholic Church. He pleaded for unity among Christians and begged the leaders of nations to settle their disputes and devote their best efforts to bringing justice and peace to the people they rule.

November 4, 1958, the feast of St. Charles Borromeo, was set as the day of coronation by the new Pope and under the glare of lights for

motion picture and television cameras, the sturdy, old pontiff went through the four-hour ceremonies and Mass without seeming to tire. On the balcony above the main entrance to St. Peter's basilica, he received the tiara and gave his blessing to Rome and to the world.

Shortly after his election, Pope John ordered the men who head various offices in the Vatican to be prepared for regular meetings with him. He made it clear that his reign would be his own and that he was not afraid of breaking with tradition of the past. He took a complete tour of the hundred and forty-one acres that make up the Vatican and surprised more than one of the office workers by walking in unannounced to visit.

One day he picked up his telephone and called the editor of the Vatican newspaper, L'Osservatore Romano. He wished to see Mr. Dalla Torre at once in his private office. The editor hurried to keep his appointment and when he returned to his office, he reported to his staff that the pope had told him not to use flowery phrases in the newspaper when referring to the pontiff's acts. "We are to write, 'The pope said this or that' and let it go at that."

Only a few days after his coronation, the new pope declared that he would create new Cardinals and increase the Sacred College to seventy-five members. This broke another tradition which stated that the College should consist of only seventy members. From the United States, Archbishop Cushing of Boston and Archbishop O'Hara, C.S.C., of Philadelphia were named Cardinals.

An old monsignor in the Vatican declined the honor of being made a cardinal by Pope John. The pope graciously agreed not to elevate him but to show his esteem for the good man, he went to him on his feast day and asked,

"Would you do me the favor of having dinner with me tonight?"

The humble monsignor was so amazed at the invitation that he was speechless for a moment. At last he found himself saying, "Of course, Your Holiness. I should be delighted to do so."

For only eight days did Pope John agree to follow the tradition that a pope must eat alone. After some scholarly research, he discovered that there was nothing in the Bible stating that a pope must eat by himself and he began the custom of inviting cardinals and friends to dine with him.

On Christmas Day, 1958, the Pope delivered a radio message to the world in which he thanked all those who had sent him congratulations on his election to the papacy, praised Pope Pius' work and pleaded again for unity among Christian peoples. Later in the day he went to visit two hospitals and enjoyed going from ward to ward smiling and talking to the children in their white beds. Everywhere he went, he was followed by photographers busy taking pictures of him. The blinding flashes exploded again and again around him until finally he turned to the newsmen to say, "I think there should be yet another work of mercy— patiently enduring people who annoy us. I like photographers," he smiled, "but I also like peace. And now, so that I will not annoy you and make you practice patience, I will stop before this becomes a long, long speech."

The photographers understood the kind hint and most of them decided they had taken enough pictures of the pontiff for that day.

On the following day, the Pope went to the Queen of Heaven prison in Rome for an hour's visit with the inmates. "Since I knew you folks could not come to see me, I decided to come to see you," he joked after his arrival.

At the beginning of his visit, the pope was taken to visit only the minor offenders, but when he insisted that he wished to see those confined because of serious crimes, the officials in charge of the prison objected. "They might harm you, Your Holiness," they cautioned.

"Nonsense!" came the reply. "Open the gates for me. I want to see those children of the Lord."

The guards obeyed and marveled that the prisoners cheered and applauded and wept as the round, little man in white came walking and talking among them. One of them knelt down and begged the pope to seek a pardon for him from the government.

"I'm afraid I have little power to do that for you," Pope John smiled kindly, "but I have some power in a much higher place. I grant you an indulgence and this I have full power to give." He blessed the kneeling man slowly and then continued his tour.

When the pontiff was ready to leave the prison, he addressed all of the inmates, humorously recalling that one of his relatives had once been put in jail for a month for hunting without a license. The incident had made a great impression on him and taught him a lesson.

Before he stepped into his car to be driven back to the Vatican, Pope John ordered the prison warden to provide a special chicken dinner on the feast of the Epiphany for all the prisoners.

"Chicken?" the warden asked.

"Send me the bill for the meal," the Pope smiled, stepping gingerly into his car. "I want my friends to have a good dinner on January 6!"

For a man in his late seventies, Pope John follows a rigorous schedule. He rises at four every morning, bathes and shaves and then prays until seven o'clock when he says Mass in his private chapel. After breakfast, he answers mail and reads the newspapers that are brought to him. Then come audiences with important people and the members of his Vatican corps. After lunch he visits the Blessed Sacrament and then works until evening at the many tasks that are his as ruler of the Church. At eight in the evening, he has his dinner and retires at ten. He says five decades of the Rosary each day— one decade for the people of each continent. As a priest, he must say the Divine Office daily, and this he recites at different times during his long, busy day.

Pope John has not forgotten the holy man who preceded him on the throne of St. Peter. He has given his approval to a prayer asking God for the beatification of Pope Pius XII and has approved the filming of the life of this pontiff.

He named Cardinal Tardini his Secretary of State and consecrated him personally with other archbishops and bishops for various sees.

Nothing is too small for his personal attention and he still delights in slipping away from his guards and motorcycle escort for visits about Rome and its suburbs. Once he vanished from his apartment and even his secretary did not know where he had gone. He was found an hour later in a rest home for old priests several miles away visiting his old friends.

When he received a letter from two altar boys in Cremona asking him to allow them to serve Mass for him, he sent back a quick reply telling them to come to Rome for the Mass and enclosing a picture of himself and a blessing for them and their families.

One of the things the Pope enjoys doing most is meeting people in private and public

audiences. After meeting the Swiss Guards for-
mally, he sat down with them and ordered tea
to be served. "We are together every day," he
smiled with a twinkle in his eye, "but we do not
have an opportunity to visit. We can become
better acquainted now."

When Sisters of Nevers dropped in for a
visit, he recalled that nuns of the Order taught
in Venice. "They expanded in different parts
of the city and finally they had to stop because,
as you know, Venice is built on the sea, and if
they had continued to grow, they would have
fallen right into the water!"

It is fortunate that the pontiff retains his
wonderful good humor and happy smile, because heavy problems weigh on his shoulders
and he works hard to find solutions for them.
Almost fifty-three million Catholics behind the
Iron Curtain are being crushed and killed by
persecution. The Church in China is falling

into schism and Catholics in Latin America desperately need priests. To bring about unity of Christians, Pope John has called a Council of the Church. As head of the Church on earth, this saintly, old man must do all in his power to bring all souls to Christ. Bishops from all parts of the world must be received in audience, their problems understood and solutions found for them. When disaster strikes unfortunate people in any land, the Pope must do all in his power to send money and aid to the afflicted. Canonizations of new saints must take place and the important feasts of the Church celebrated splendidly in the great basilicas of the Eternal City.

Pope John XXIII needs God's help in his difficult work and he needs the prayers of all men of good will. The shepherd who once led the sheep to the south pasture near Sotto il Monte now leads millions of souls closer to their eternal home. May God grant him a long and glorious reign on earth and a great reward in heaven when his work is finally finished!

The End

CPSIA information can be obtained
at www.ICGtesting.com
Printed in the USA
BVHW051529080223
658099BV00010B/495

9 781258 496340